HOUSEWORK

SUSAN BIRCHENOUGH

KFS
PAMPHLETS

NEWTON-LE-WILLOWS

Published in the United Kingdom in 2018
by The Knives Forks And Spoons Press,
51 Pipit Avenue,
Newton-le-Willows,
Merseyside,
WA12 9RG.

ISBN 978-1-912211-12-8

Acknowledgments:

Several of the poems from this collection have appeared elsewhere: 'Matisse on the Southbank' featured in M58; 'I'm Bed', in Ink Sweat and Tears; 'Footnotes' & 'Left Luggage', in Red Ceilings; 'Billie Holiday and Friends', 'Billie Holiday', 'I Like' & 'Acoustics' were anthologised in Yesterday's Music Today, which was edited by Mike Ferguson and Rupert Loydell. I would like to thank these editors for supporting my work.

Cover image by Olga Bondarenko.

Supported using public funding by

ARTS COUNCIL
ENGLAND

Table of Contents

housework	7
left luggage	10
Billie Holiday and friends	11
acoustics	12
I like	13
brainwaves	14
jubilee footbridge	15
down a side street	16
I saw it	17
footnotes	18
sunday	19
matisse on the southbank	20
et cetera	21
silver screen	22
mist	23
blue sky thinking	24
times new roman	26
the word is sexy	27
I'm bed	28
i am 0	29

HOUSEWORK

housework

(permanently   shelling   peas ... and   occasionally
tasting one)

morning opens listless to-do's
Thomas the Tank was on them
rooves gleam the white smell of flattening cotton

bleary, crumpled
a postbox hit your bloody eye

red primary ran laughing hometime

wi   wi   wi   DOW
through window
propriety gone graciously to seed
(not the Gothic tart on the hill, though)

tea lifts out the tyranny of days   months   years

I'm still in the attic
now I pay rent

creeps in a petty place from 9 till 5

you ok?
I can hear the sleep in your voice

sorry ... I wasn't thinking ... about Saturday night ... and
you being out
that's ok ... no worries ... see you

Thatcher's morose eye in the grain

rain
hygienically cleans using the power of nature

Osama bin ... cluttered and on empty
today hoovers

puree packet Pisa
4 scrunchpools in cellophane

fingertips

he liked it with soy sauce

it's length of fermentation
that's what counts
not that cheap stuff
like the bread

soybean bandwagon

dogma
dogged by bloody dogma
dogma: derivation dog
wonder
is it in our bones ... or in the water ?

fuck him
fuck it

next !

the comedy of why runs down the window
through my hair the why the fuck after I'd

drips tomorrow and tomorrow

mould that wasn't there

in Croatia
local people
have
only had
bad
experiences
with caves

left luggage

future is
   over
        there
  in my gut
    within
      fingertips
        stretch out
            out beyond
             I know
             an other
             some days
                far corner
        corner   right moment
             before
             tongue's tip on
             step by ...
                in front of
              shoulder
            broad shoulder

Billie Holiday and friends

papapaaaarpapapapa
   prup papapaaar

blaaaaaaaackandwhite

blaaablaaablaaaackandwhiiiiite

blaaaackandbluuuue blackaaandbluuue

  prup prup papapapapaaaaaar

blaaaackandblueblaaaackandblueblaaaaaaandbluuuuuue
 preep preeee pryeepryee preep preep

preeeeeeeeeeeeeeeep

blaaaack andwhiite   blaaaack   andwhiiiiite

blaaaaaaaackandbluuuuuue

acoustics

you've unplugged
the acoustic   is
diff   er   ent

my breath

I

the dis   tance between walls

creaking   is
but your chair   isn't

under my skin   you   singing

I like

I like my jazz   not to be   too   free
to flap   inthebreeze
                  then be caught   just
at the   edge
with a sti   tching that's not quite a seam
but sometimes   is
a roughmus   cular c/hord
brass braid
or fine twine twisted   embroiders
                discovers   new
      patterns   predestinedin
      braintap   estry

      brain waves because
      theyalreadyknew

      the man is gone
      a reflecting on   the instrument
      it screams   it frets a light and dark
                    wroughts an iron
            gilds a lilly
jigs a perfect puzzlement
then leaves him   standing

brainwaves

a skull I could crush in my fingers

and later   I'd already be in bed

from there   to a victorian one   with gristle

ment ad just.   ad just ment.   ad ment just

just ad ment   *ad* just ment   *just* ment ad.   ad ment just

ment ad just   ad just *ment*

next summer   *i promise*

this isn't the same as.   *this isn't the same as*

sometimes when it rings

well....................that's often the case

jubilee footbridge

duhduh's over hungerford

     chupchurping

          a breeze

        snatches   bambam of a rap

rhubarbarbing

      duh duh

   bambamBAMing

      migrating

        acrossing

    the zebra noon sun

down a side street

down a side street   it finds me
tilting above an old fireplace
half pissed   with a twist of
clenching of shoulders

no . . . that would be . . . no . . . *is*   the urinal
the urinal is false on so many levels

is it mostly bull?

later,   the lift is complex

just to be
a ful   filled lift
a smooth operator
is not enough

the carpet is soft with silences

he sits motionless on the little stage where the curves of poetry edge –
a distortion, merely
in a tattooing flow of text

I saw it
[manchester]

it rumbles above me when
i walk on portland street
and in 1910 when
a man is pushing a handcart

i saw it down a side street when
i was beginning to know the city and i went alone
down back streets to st annes the way you had
shown me when
and we were holding hands and you told me they had
made that building jump when

upstairs on a bus on oxford road I look up at it for when
and see the little roof temple when
your arm is round my shoulder and I'm thinking what
bonkers things they liked to put on rooftops when

I saw it when
the harmonica player flew in from spain and packed
the pews and it was hot and everyone was happy and
the shopping lay unwanted and the gold and red and
blue and it had been one of just two churches when

footnotes

1. this pure Labour lineage   But far more influential
was the power of commerce to deliver the
free-market

gothic was architecture convinced it could influence.
It was infused   It became untethered
later it was adopted, for romantic reasons

when Victoria was on the throne, movements often
arose

2. there's a lot of it
I know more of some of it than you
you know more of some of it than me

3.   paint brown trickling steam
runs into mosaic breaks ov
er time drops off in little pla
stic curls gunge compresse
d death from the softening
rigid silent long ing to melt
on deep searching tongues

(i) black gunge compressed death(sheet) mimics deathrings millimetres thin

(ii) sloshing ecstacy of easy greed

4. I can see you, DOOR !

sunday

backlit in orange sunday when the grey wind city
buildings even pigeons aren't up for it
spicey snooze a bit the booze in moderation
hot and ginger last night cold today

matisse on the south bank

something about the sword swallower reminds me of
maybe: warmleanbonebeardgrown, spilt a cup of hot tea -
the blisters took weeks to get right, she tells me

the carriage fills up like streets
the window is spattered but speed's only fun if you feel it

damp sun
torn gritstone
: "mum"

et cetera
[buxton]

oh let me count the ways

i don't feel like smiling a whispered resilience of trees

up here

spooked you out with the moon stillness of poppies

who is she with wings and no knickers

is she an angel

of war

a sword makes you heroes

for her

is she an angel

of death

softly on your mess of flesh who'll never use your dick again

if you ever did except in brothels in France and you

didn't want it to be this way when you wrote home

is she your old bloodied country

always 20

or is her blank look

of an angel

while the raining of sea

the arthritic town   eating soup

with the smell of wood and plush

carpets where

the faint scratchy voice of queen mary

have a nice day.   (strapped to a board)

have a nice day   (unable to breathe)

silver screen
[Billie Holiday]

hats
sophisti   fags
in fingers   greased back
gardenias

maniquined
in unflesh
soft and hard
and texture
tweed and satin
velvet

what does the light say
bright
and reflecting away

why don't it tell

why do I see a Warhol print

impossibly

and devoid

mist

mist

5 trees

2 chimneys

1 roof

birds
I hear   but can't see

trees   perfectly still

sweating

the fire of spring

blue sky thinking

the hills ache through pylons
and across the blue lips of caves

a bent-back tree remembers
and softly weeps out the storm

the bulldog stare of new development
tarmac   and   concrete   unfamiliar   to   rivers'   soft   syllables

the tiny house at the scrag end remembers
at the drop of a hat it will tell you Great Ant May and in
my faytha's faytha's time
anecdotal only
and mildly amusing
or interesting if you think finding your roots will add value
usually you take the car so don't bump into
except maybe on a Sunday if the weather's fine
and something primeval thinks of legs
or possibly the supplement said
under the heading tips for healthy living
try to get a little exercise
and it's wise to sometimes walk
and at a push there's time before they come round for dinner
and that deal that makes you flutter –
and that's another thing –
your heart
Tom said he'd looked and reckoned it 'd be a good investment
with new windows and the back knocked out and through
with lots of character and a large conservatory added
wasn't that a few drops?
drop off Jenny later

raw red twigs in the garden
the house stretches pinstripe legs
settles for the evening
an owl shrieks above the yellow skylight

there's outdoor TV there so you can take the summer air
and keep the bloke and kids happy and she won't miss her soap
all in for a fiver

a rook twists mid-air
dives hopeful
above the junction a blue galliard is dancing

flat slug shadow slithers over hills

the sun remembers dancing with the leaves
the sun remembers the rising heartbeat of drums

the hills lumber by
road scratches its itch
town fidgets

times new roman

a dull ache
a bone ache
where love has healed
become congealed
love

his texts look a surgically clean no nonsense edge

i hold my love in
controlled
clinical
conditions
to minimise
blood loss

the word is sexy

the word is **SeX**y

it **SprawlS** on white **SHeetS**

KicKing and

OPening

where everything is blac**K** and white

Page 2 fo**LLO**w**S** on from **Page 1**

with n**O** me**SS**

it effortle**SS**ly conform**S**

to n**O**tion**S** of beauty

at **LeaS**t on the **SurfaCe**

it **LieS** f**L**at without crea**S**ing

ZZZ SLeePing

it **SmeLLS** of c**L**arity

and **S**tuff you **SH**ould be**L**ieve in

it**S** tongue f**L**ic**KS** and **SyLabulateS**

it **PunCtuateS**

in the **S**oft   white   **SPaCeS**   you glim**PS**e   the grey**S**

I'm bed

I'm bed
not wardrobe with my back against the wall

ladle not fork
breast stroke not crawl
lintel not brick
flagpole not vault
sweetcorn not wheat

I would like to meet a man   for swimming,
visits to Ikea,
soup,
who
prefers public buildings to a pub (lol)
and is looking to buy a cottage   in a year or two

gluten intolerance   would be a plus

i am 0

(a)

i am 1 of many 1's
and i am also 0
i don't count
as an individual
unless i joke that i
would like
to strangle cameron
and then
i might be
1
if i make the joke
a significant number of times to people who agree
they can see right through me
because i'm 0
i'm just 1
in a million
other 1's
with 0
to protect me

(b)

i am
cracked
open
to read
the easy flow
of arteries that keep me alive

each beat of my heart
is mummified

i hang in glass jars
to be scrutinized